MW01226501

1

Vesta Within: 30 Days with you

By
The Loon

This book is dedicated to all
that finds themselves lost at some
point in their life. It doesn't
matter the reason that has caused
you to feel this way. It could be
due to your heart being broken one
too many times or spirit
questioning so many questions. Or
you are just simply tired. I
dedicate this book and the next 30
days to you. These thirty days are
dedicated to you.

Hello There Stranger!

Hello, there stranger! I say stranger because if you picked up this book, you probably feel like a stranger in your skin. Right now you probably don't recognize the person you see in the mirror. Trust me I know the feeling. I have been there several times throughout my life. Which is the reason I have written this book.

Disclaimer

Let me get the disclaimer out of the way. Under NO circumstance do I claim to be a medical professional. Nor do I have any degree within the psychological field. Why do I feel that I can write the book? I feel I could write this book because I have been at that point where I have been broken. I have been at that point where I wanted to raise my hands and give up completely. Despite feeling this way I found a way to get through it. Granted like everything in life this is a method that has to be consistent but I know that I'm not alone with such moments. Some of us make it. Many of us struggle. Unfortunately, some don't make it. I hope what I share within these pages will help bring up the numbers of those that make it. If anything helps you find your hope.

This book is not the ultimate fix. If you thought that's what this book was, I'm sorry to disappoint. The best way to approach this book is as a stepping stone. A stepping stone to get you out of your rut. A stepping stone to your next emotional step. If you honestly think about it, any self-help book or video that you pick up is just that. A stepping stone.

Why use self-talk?

I am sure that you have heard the term self-talk within different sources. You talk to so many different people daily. You provide them with encouraging words. You try to provide them with sound advice. If you put some thought into it, how often do you do that for yourself? How often do you give yourself the same positive advice? How often do you give yourself the same encouraging words that you give to others? If you can't say that you have to these questions and mean it. That's the problem. We have gotten so caught up or in the habit of pleasing others, that we have completely forgotten about the one individual that should truly matter. You! Now please don't get me wrong. This book doesn't support the notion that it's all about you and screw everyone else. NO! That is not what this book is about. If that is what you are expecting, you will be highly disappointed. This book is about you. It's about you reconnecting with the you that you know you can be. It's about developing a healthy mental health state that is supportive of you.

The way this book Works

There are a few rules that go with this book. You will

need a few items and tasks to be performed.

- You will need a mirror.
- You will start a journal. (That's if you don't already have one.)
- You will need to put in the effort. (You will be cheating and shortchanging no one but you.)

Your Participation

To get the full effect of this book there are a few things you will need to do. Hopefully, these will get you into some healthy habits.

- You will need a journal. (It's a nice way to keep track of progress and for you to look back at later dates.)
- The three daily conversations **will** have to occur in the front of

a mirror.

- Remember that you have to be completely honest with what you journal. (You are only cheating yourself if you're not honest. If it's too much to write at the time simply write that you will revisit later. And do so when you feel comfortable.)
- Please curtail the suggested conversations to your liking. Yet still have these conversations in front of a mirror.
- It helps to read the additions to each day to assist you on a daily basis. For those moments that may happen to you when you least expect it.

It Works As Well As You Put In

I need to say that you get out of this book as much as you put into it. Let me say that again. You get out into this as much as you put into yourself. How much do you want to reunite with who you truly are? This truly depends completely on you. You have to ask yourself how much do you want to put into this. I can only say if you apply for the work you will get results. Keep in mind that this is in everything in life. Before you can apply it externally, let's apply internally. Who is more important to you but you. Let's get to know you again.

<u>Day 1</u>

Welcome to the first day and your first step toward you returning to you. **YOU** are about to reclaim who you know you can be. **YOU** are about to reclaim your spirit. **YOU** are returning to your heart. **YOU** are reclaiming your strength. Are you ready to reclaim **YOU**?

On this first day, I would like to share a brief part of myself with you. This is a journey I embarked on completely by accident. I found myself in a place where I felt spiritually broken and drained. My heart was so broken and bruised that I couldn't see any healing insight. I couldn't even find hope at the bottom of Pandora's Box. I couldn't find joy within any aspect of my life. Even the parts that should use too. There might have been a smile on my face but it wasn't genuine. I couldn't even look into a mirror

without my stomach turning upside
down. In a matter of fact, I did
everything in my power to avoid
them. (This was mostly since I
wasn't happy with my appearances,
but more so the person looking back
at me. I truly didn't recognize
her.) For this reason, I have
required that you have the three
main conversations in front of a
mirror. Any size mirror will work.
If you want to start small, start
with a pocket mirror, then work
yourself up. It may be
uncomfortable at first but remember
that this is part of the process of
becoming more familiar with you.
***Remember to have this
conversation in front of a
mirror.***

Daily Conversations

Morning Conversation:

Hello you! I've
missed you so much. It's been so
lonely without you. I missed your
hair.
I hope you know it's perfect in
every way.

When was the last time
you genuinely smiled at the world?
Today is the day that you
will allow your smile to shine. I
would like to welcome you back.
You're going
to be wonderful today.

Midday Conversation:

How are you holding up?
How did your morning go?
I want to remind you that there
is no such thing as a perfect day.
Despite not having "the" perfect
day (so far).
I'm looking at the beautiful
placement of your hair.
You can't get better than that.
I'm going to show you how
wonderful you are:

***List all that went
well in the morning. (Keep in mind
there is nothing too small to add
to this list.)***

Evening Conversation:

Wow! Didn't you have a
beautiful and productive day!

12

No day is perfect but this day
still went well.
That's all you could ask for.
Today you had the following go
your way:

***List all the positive
things you learned today. ***

Additional Conversations:

When Faced With a Difficult
Situation

I know this seems like a serious
challenge or block.
You can handle this. Take a
moment. Take a breath.
Center yourself!
Take a look at all your options.
Look at your options. Which one
is best applied with the best
results? You can make the right
decision. You got this!

When you feel you can't do this

You knew this wasn't going to be
easy.
You chose to go down this road
for a reason.

You made the right choice.
You know that right? You got
this. You can push through this.
You got this!

Before Taking on too much

Okay! You know you want to help
everyone.
You also want to go everywhere
with all your friends.
If you do that when will you
have time for yourself?
If your commitment to this will
you be over-extending yourself?

When Faced With Doubt

You know that it's so much
easier not to do this.
But you know that not doing this
will not make you happy.
You have become accustomed to
looking in the mirror.
You love the person looking back
at you. How can you go back?
You can do this. You are better
than you were yesterday.
You refuse to go back.

14

Day 2

       Your eyes have opened up to a beautiful day. You have woken up one day closer to you that is more recognizable. Remember that as you embark on this day. Yes, that is what I said. Know that you are in the progress of reclaiming valuable real estate within your mind. When I originally tried to climb out of the hole that I found myself in, it took a while before I realized that I had squatters in my mind. I was preoccupied with irreverent situations that had nothing to do with the benefit of my mental health. All occupying space in my mind for free. Due to this complication, I have added some additional conversations that I hope assist you during some of the more challenging moments that may occur during your day. I do suggest doing this in front of a mirror but it's not mandatory for

these additions. We can't predict
what will occur at any given moment
on any given day. That's the reason
I have these additional
conversations, to act as a
countermeasure. There will be
moments where you won't be able to
get in front of a mirror. In those
times I encourage you to mentally
have those particular conversations
to memory, or something similar.
Your daily conversation should be
conducted in front of a mirror.

Daily Conversations:

Morning Conversations:

Hello, Wonderful! You
have made it to another beautiful
day.
Look at how perfectly those
eyebrows lay over your eyes.
Perfect hair,
Perfect eyebrows.
Look at you.
Ready to shine your light upon
the world.
You are wonderful in every way.
From the strands on the top of
your head right down to your toes.

16

You got this day.
Go get'em.

Midday Conversation:

You are halfway through
this day.
Let's take a look at what you
did right this morning.
You have done the following
successfully:
***List all that went
well in the morning. ***

Evening Conversation:

You have made it through
another day.
You have made it through your
misgivings and have made it through
so many more of your successes.
You understand and accept this.
Today we learned the following
about ourselves:
***List all the positive
things you learned today. ***

Additional Conversations:

When Faced With a Difficult
Situation

17

I know this seems like a serious
challenge or block.
You can handle this. Take a
moment. Take a breath.
Center yourself!
Take a look at all your options.
Look at your options. Which one
is best applied with the best
results? You can make the right
decision. You got this!

When you feel you can't do this

You knew this wasn't going to be
easy.
You chose to go down this road
for a reason.
You made the right choice.
You know that right? You got
this. You can push through this.
You got this!

Before Taking on too much

Okay! You know you want to help
everyone.
You also want to go everywhere
with all your friends.
If you do that when will you
have time for yourself?

If your commitment to this will
you be over-extending yourself?

When Faced With Doubt

You know that it's so much
easier not to do this.
But you know that not doing this
will not make you happy.
You have become accustomed to
looking in the mirror.
You love the person looking back
at you. How can you go back?
You can do this. You are better
than you were yesterday.
You refuse to go back.

Day 3

      Look at that! You have
woken up to another day. A day that
is full of so much potential. I
know that morning can be hard at
times but the day always holds
great moments. Why so great? Your
wonderfully beautiful eyes opened
up on this day. Another day for you
to shine your light. Yes, indeed,
you don't know what the day holds.
I add this on this day because this
is usually around the time when
doubt tries to slip into your mind
and stop you from moving on. This
day usually is your defining
moment. This is the day that you
decide to either throw your hands
up and give or you decide that
enough is enough and nothing is
going to stop you from being you.
Starting on this day I have added
an addition for your evening
journal. You will be given the

chance to take account of any
difficult situations that may have
come up during your day and how you
dealt with them. If you couldn't at
the moment journal how you would
have liked to handle it. This will
give you a chance to prepare any
for any future obstacles that you
will face. Remember. Keep going!
Don't give up! Just know whatever
happens - You will shine!

Daily Conversations:

Morning Conversation:

You got up today.
Your eyes hold so much depth
within them.
They are so captivating as they
sit underneath those wonderful
eyebrows.
You are showing up!
You are ready for another
fulfilling day.
You have success within your
sights.

Midday Conversation:

So far you have been

21

present for every moment today.
Even though not every experience
has been pleasant.
You have accepted your
experiences as a blessing.
You have experienced the
following today:
***List all that went
well in the morning. ***

Evening Conversation:

You did great today.
You shined through today.
You made it through every
obstacle that was placed before
you.
You have had some wonderful
moments.
You also hit a few obstacles.
You still made it through.
Today you learned the
following about yourself:
***List all the positive
things you learned today. ***

You also had the
following difficult moments:
***List what provided a
challenge for you and how you
handled it.***

Additional Conversations:

When Faced With a Difficult Situation

I know this seems like a serious
challenge or block.
You can handle this. Take a
moment. Take a breath.
Center yourself!
Take a look at all your options.
Look at your options. Which one
is best applied with the best
results? You can make the right
decision. You got this!

When you feel you can't do this

You knew this wasn't going to be
easy.
You chose to go down this road
for a reason.
You made the right choice.
You know that right? You got
this. You can push through this.
You got this!

Before Taking on too much

Okay! You know you want to help

everyone.
You also want to go everywhere
with all your friends.
If you do that when will you
have time for yourself?
If your commitment to this will
you be over-extending yourself?

When Faced With Doubt

You know that it's so much
easier not to do this.
But you know that not doing this
will not make you happy.
You have become accustomed to
looking in the mirror.
You love the person looking back
at you. How can you go back?
You can do this. You are better
than you were yesterday.
You refuse to go back.

Day 4

Every day that you wake upholds the potential for another exciting day. Every day you wake up is filled with the anticipation of the unknown. This is your journey. Your journey back to you. I know it sometimes seems hard but you can do this. You can't control everything that will occur on this day or any day for that matter. Remember that you can only control how you react and deal with what comes your way. Remember to do the following when those challenges arise:

- Take a moment
- Take a breath
- Remember you can handle anything.

Daily Conversations:

Morning Conversation:

Hello Beautiful!
Your nose lays perfectly on your
face.
It brings wonderful attention to
those eyes, eyebrows, and that
hair. You got this!
You are amazing in every way.
Straighten that back and look to
the sky.
You know no limits.

Midday Conversation:

So far you're doing
great.
You have made it halfway through
this day.
You handled yourself like a pro.
Keep it up!
You accomplished the following:
***List all that went
well in the morning. ***

Evening Conversation:

You made it through
another beautiful day.
Remember that you are a
superstar.

You learned the following today:
***List all the positive things you learned today. ***

You were even able to handle those difficult moments:
List what provided a challenge for you and how you handled it.

Additional Conversations:

When Faced With a Difficult Situation

I know this seems like a serious challenge or block.
You can handle this. Take a moment. Take a breath.
Center yourself!
Take a look at all your options.
Look at your options. Which one is best applied with the best results? You can make the right decision. You got this!

When you feel you can't do this

You knew this wasn't going to be easy.
You chose to go down this road

27

for a reason.
You made the right choice.
You know that right? You got
this. You can push through this.
You got this!

Before Taking on too much

Okay! You know you want to help
everyone.
You also want to go everywhere
with all your friends.
If you do that when will you
have time for yourself?
If your commitment to this will
you be over-extending yourself?

When Faced With Doubt

You know that it's so much
easier not to do this.
But you know that not doing this
will not make you happy.
You have become accustomed to
looking in the mirror.
You love the person looking back
at you. How can you go back?
You can do this. You are better
than you were yesterday.
You refuse to go back.

28

Day 5

How are you feeling, so far? How does your skin feel so far? To be honest, it's a bit too early to feel completely comfortable in your skin. Keep in mind that you are only on Day 5. You didn't get to this state overnight. It took time to get to this point. (although it snuck up on you) within that same light, it will take time for you to get back on track. So don't you give up. Something for you to keep in mind is that you speak to everyone else. You encourage so many people within your life. So why is it so hard for you to speak to yourself? Why is it hard for you to speak to yourself in the loving and caring manner that you deserve? Your self-talk is crucial during this exercise. Be kind to yourself. Speak kindly to yourself. You're doing great!

Daily Conversations:

Morning Conversation:

Hello Warrior! Look at
that beautiful smile this morning.
Look at you bringing your "A"
game today.
Look at how far you have come in
such a short time.
You are a Rock Star.
You keep going with the flow.
Shine your light bright today.
Shine your light with a smile on
your face.

Midday Conversation:

How are you holding up?
You've made it halfway through
this day.
Do you know how much of a
rewarding day it is for you so far?
You are so slaying it. You have
accomplished the following so far:
***List all that went
well in the morning. ***

Evening Conversation:

You have reached another
day to put in the books.
You know that there is no such
thing as a completely easy day but
you warrior through it.
All the while with that
wonderful smile on your face.
Today you learned the
following:
***List all the positive
things you learned today. ***

Today you had difficulty
with the following:
***List what provided a
challenge for you and how you
handled it.***

Additional Conversations:

When Faced With a Difficult Situation

I know this seems like a serious
challenge or block.
You can handle this. Take a
moment. Take a breath.
Center yourself!
Take a look at all your options.
Look at your options. Which one

is best applied with the best
results? You can make the right
decision. You got this!

When you feel you can't do this

You knew this wasn't going to be
easy.
You chose to go down this road
for a reason.
You made the right choice.
You know that right? You got
this. You can push through this.
You got this!

Before Taking on too much

Okay! You know you want to help
everyone.
You also want to go everywhere
with all your friends.
If you do that when will you
have time for yourself?
If your commitment to this will
you be over-extending yourself?

When Faced With Doubt

You know that it's so much
easier not to do this.

But you know that not doing this
will not make you happy.
You have become accustomed to
looking in the mirror.
You love the person looking back
at you. How can you go back?
You can do this. You are better
than you were yesterday.
You refuse to go back.

Day 6

Each one of us has our ways of dealing with the different types of stresses that come our way. These are our coping mechanisms. These methods come from our survival instinct. At times these methods can be healthy, yet in the same light more often than most those methods could be counterproductive. Which could be quite damaging. Just take a moment to think about it the way that you deal with your stress. Which category does your coping method fall under? Could it be your current coping methods got you to this point where you find yourself in need? This is just food for thought as you come closer to the end of your first seven days.

Daily Conversations:

Morning Conversation:

Hello Love!
How are you doing so far?
I am looking at one fabulous face.
That beautiful face is lovingly perfect.
It is one day closer to hitting your week mark.
You should be extremely proud of yourself.
You should show the world how proud you are of that oh-so-beautiful face.
Go out there and shine.

Midday Conversation:

You will have your good days and you will have your bad days. What type of day are you having?
Let's bring your focus to the positive you.
Did you realize that you have accomplished so much so far?
***List all that went well in the morning. ***

Evening Conversation:

No matter what has happened throughout this day, try to keep in mind that you went through this day beautifully. You have shown such grace today. This is what you have learned today:
***List all the positive things you learned today. ***

You had some trouble with the following:
List what provided a challenge for you and how you handled it.

Additional Conversations:

When Faced With a Difficult Situation

I know this seems like a serious challenge or block.
You can handle this. Take a moment. Take a breath.
Center yourself!
Take a look at all your options. Look at your options. Which one is best applied with the best

results? You can make the right
decision. You got this!

When you feel you can't do this

You knew this wasn't going to be
easy.
You chose to go down this road
for a reason.
You made the right choice.
You know that right? You got
this. You can push through this.
You got this!

Before Taking on too much

Okay! You know you want to help
everyone.
You also want to go everywhere
with all your friends.
If you do that when will you
have time for yourself?
If your commitment to this will
you be over-extending yourself?

When Faced With Doubt

You know that it's so much
easier not to do this.
But you know that not doing this

will not make you happy.
You have become accustomed to
looking in the mirror.
You love the person looking back
at you. How can you go back?
You can do this. You are better
than you were yesterday.
You refuse to go back.

Day 7

Congratulations! You have made it through an entire week of coming closer to the you that you know you can be. This past week has brought you that much closer. I would suggest that you treat yourself to this wonderful accomplishment. It doesn't matter how small the celebration is. Take some time today to celebrate with you. Go ahead. Take yourself out. Partake on what brings a smile to your face. If there is anyone who deserves it, it is you.

Daily Conversations:

Morning Conversation:

Man! You are amazing.
Look at you.
With your perfect curves.
They fall into the perfect places.

You have knocked out a
difficult, yet quite a productive
week.
Now, look at you.
Ready to take on one more
day.
Remember, you got this.

Midday Conversation:

You're halfway through
the day.
How do you feel?
Let's see where you're at.
This morning you accomplish the
following:
***List all that went
well in the morning. ***

Evening Conversation:

Do you know that you're
amazing?
Do you know why?
You have reached the end of your
week.
You are that much closer to
being reunited with you.
Wish I could give you a
huge hug.
Let's see what you have learned

today:
***List all the positive
things you learned today. ***

You had difficulty with
the following:
***List what provided a
challenge for you and how you
handled it.***

Additional Conversations:

When Faced With a Difficult Situation

I know this seems like a serious
challenge or block.
You can handle this. Take a
moment. Take a breath.
Center yourself!
Take a look at all your options.
Look at your options. Which one
is best applied with the best
results? You can make the right
decision. You got this!

When you feel you can't do this

You knew this wasn't going to be
easy.
You chose to go down this road

for a reason.
You made the right choice.
You know that right? You got
this. You can push through this.
You got this!

Before Taking on too much

Okay! You know you want to help
everyone.
You also want to go everywhere
with all your friends.
If you do that when will you
have time for yourself?
If your commitment to this will
you be over-extending yourself?

When Faced With Doubt

You know that it's so much
easier not to do this.
But you know that not doing this
will not make you happy.
You have become accustomed to
looking in the mirror.
You love the person looking back
at you. How can you go back?
You can do this. You are better
than you were yesterday.
You refuse to go back.

Intermission

First I would like to
congratulate you on making it
through your first seven days. You
made it through a whole week. You
can't truly fathom how wonderful
this accomplishment is. You are
turning things around. I know that
these last few days have been quite
challenging. It has even been
emotionally challenging at times.
We can face so many different
obstacles head-on in this life, yet
time and time again it's always the
hardest thing to face head-on is
ourselves.

I named this chapter
"intermission", to allow yourself…
better yet give yourself permission
to take a breath and celebrate your
wonderful accomplishments. If you
need it or desire to do so. If you
choose to take a breather, please
try not to fall back habit of
negative thinking. You have come

too far to fall back on bad habits.
Take this moment to enjoy the
moments of this day instead.

Keep rocking it!

Day 8

Welcome Back! Are you ready to start your second week of getting closer to you? Please take a moment and realize how you viewed yourself in the mirror for the last seven days. Look at your accomplishments. Accept them. Take pride in it. Look at your shortcomings. Accept them. Know that you will overcome them. This upcoming week will be more of a team effort. Don't forget! We got this and we are going to get through another seven days. We are going to reclaim more of that real estate within our minds.

Daily Conversations:

Morning Conversation:

Hello! My! My! My!
Let's take a look at that
beautiful hair.
It's growing beautifully.

45

Look at us!
We are ready to take on the
world.
We are so ready for another
fabulous day.
We got this.
We are so going to knock this
day out.

Midday Conversation:

Let's take a deep breath
together.
We have to put ourselves through
this hump.
So far we have the following to
be proud of.
***List all that went
well in the morning. ***

Evening Conversation:

Look at us!
We made it through another
wonderful day.
We put our best foot forward and
got the best out of today.
We learned the following today!
***List all the positive
things you learned today. ***

46

We had difficulty with
the following:
***List what provided a
challenge for you and how you
handled it.***

Additional Conversations:

When Faced With a Difficult
Situation

We know this seems like a
serious challenge or block.
We can handle this. Take a
moment. Take a breath.
Let's center ourselves!
Take a look at all our options.
Look at our options. Which one
is best applied with the best
results? We can make the right
decision. We got this!

When you feel you can't do this

We knew this wasn't going to be
easy.
We chose to go down this road
for a reason.
We made the right choice.
You know that right? We got
this. We can push through this. We

got this!

Before Taking on too much

Okay! We want to help everyone.
We also want to go everywhere
    with all our friends.
If we do that when will we have
        time for us?
If we commit to this will we be
    over-extending ourselves?

When Faced With Doubt

We know that it's so much easier
        not to do this.
But we know that not doing this
    will not make us happy.
We have become accustomed to
    looking in the mirror.
We love the person looking back
at us. How can we go back?
We can do this. We are better
    than we were yesterday.
    We refuse to go back.

Day 9

        Today is the ninth day of this journey for us. We are doing great, I know that we have had a few hiccups here and there. There have even been some difficulties that we have faced daily. Are you feeling more comfortable with your self-talk? How does it feel dealing with you? I hope you are becoming more familiar with yourself. On this ninth day, I would like to propose a challenge for you. It's nothing major but it's upping your game. So far we have simply faced and dealt with our negative self-talk daily. This doesn't mean you have mastered it but I know by now that you should be feeling more comfortable with your positive self-talk. While you have gone through the steps within these past eight days, I am sure you have put some thought into the dreams and what you wanted for yourself in the past. Well in the next few days I would like to encourage you to

write down those things. Just place
them in your journal. Now the
conversations won't exactly reflect
this list but you will have a
chance to develop this list.
Remember you are taking the steps
to become you, you know you are.
Just a note, during this week I
will be using the word "we" a lot.
I am not referencing you and me.
Unfortunately, I can't take this
journey with you. I reference you
and the person in the mirror.
Remember I said this week will be a
team effort.

Daily Conversations:

Morning Conversation:

Well Hello!
Those eyebrows are looking extra
special this morning.
That hair accents it
wonderfully.
We are fabulous!
We woke up today ready to take
on the world.
We can adjust and face no matter
what comes our way.

We are a fiery beast.
We got this.

Midday Conversation:

We are completely aware
that making changes isn't always
comfortable.
We still got this and we know
it.
Let's take a look at how
our day is going so far.
***List all that went
well in the morning. ***

Evening Conversation:

We have completed another
day.
We made it through this
beautiful day.
Today showed us that we can take
on anything.
Today we learned the following:
***List all the positive
things you learned today. ***

We had a hard time with
the following:
***List what provided a

challenge for you and how you handled it. ***

Additional Conversations:

When Faced With a Difficult Situation

We know this seems like a
serious challenge or block.
We can handle this. Take a
moment. Take a breath.
Let's center ourselves!
Take a look at all our options.
Look at our options. Which one
is best applied with the best
results? We can make the right
decision. We got this!

When you feel you can't do this

We knew this wasn't going to be
easy.
We chose to go down this road
for a reason.
We made the right choice.
You know that right? We got

this. We can push through this. We
got this!

Before Taking on too much

Okay! We want to help everyone.
We also want to go everywhere
with all our friends.
If we do that when will we have
time for us?
If we commit to this will we be
over-extending ourselves?

When Faced With Doubt

We know that it's so much easier
not to do this.
But we know that not doing this
will not make us happy.
We have become accustomed to
looking in the mirror.
We love the person looking back
at us. How can we go back?
We can do this. We are better
than we were yesterday.
We refuse to go back.

Day 10

       You woke up to another beautiful day. I know by now you have discovered so much about yourself that you love. Let me reword that, you have rediscovered so much about yourself that you love. In that same light, there have been some things that you discovered that can use some adjusting. That's perfectly okay. There isn't one person that is walking this Earth that is perfect. The beautiful thing is that you realize that it's not too late to adjust accordingly. I would like to challenge you to make a list. Make a list of things you would like to improve in yourself. Remember you are just making a list. There will be more to come later on.

Daily Conversations:

54

Morning Conversation:

Look at us.
Look into those eyes.
Those glowingly beautiful eyes.
Looking forward to another
beautiful day, just waiting for us.
Let's go and do this.

Midday Conversation:

We are doing great so
far.
The opinions of others don't
matter.
We are still doing great.
So far we have the following
going for us:
***List all that went
well for you this morning.***

Evening Conversation:

We are so awesome!
Seriously, look how we made it
through this day.
We are so rocking it.
No matter the frustration.
No matter the wondrous
accomplishments.

55

We still rocked this day.
This is what went well for us:
***List all the positive
things you learned today. ***

This is what we have had
trouble with:
***List what provided a
challenge for you and how you
handled it.***

Additional Conversations:

When Faced With a Difficult Situation

We know this seems like a
serious challenge or block.
We can handle this. Take a
moment. Take a breath.
Let's center ourselves!
Take a look at all our options.
Look at our options. Which one
is best applied with the best
results? We can make the right
decision. We got this!

When you feel you can't do this

We knew this wasn't going to be
easy.

We chose to go down this road
for a reason.
We made the right choice.
You know that right? We got
this. We can push through this. We
got this!

Before Taking on too much

Okay! We want to help everyone.
We also want to go everywhere
with all our friends.
If we do that when will we have
time for us?
If we commit to this will we be
over-extending ourselves?

When Faced With Doubt

We know that it's so much easier
not to do this.
But we know that not doing this
will not make us happy.
We have become accustomed to
looking in the mirror.
We love the person looking back
at us. How can we go back?
We can do this. We are better
than we were yesterday.
We refuse to go back.

Day 11

Wow! We have another wonderful day to look forward to. We have officially made it to Day 11. Most don't make it this far. It's time to celebrate you. Now that we are done celebrating, let's take a moment to start our day.

Daily Conversations:

Morning Conversation:

Wow! Aren't we so
wonderful?
Look at the way that our noses
sit on our faces.
It's too cute for words.
Perfect.
We are so ready to take on
another day.
Remember no matter what this day
throws at us.

- We got this!

Midday Conversation:

We are tearing it up
today.
We are on fire.
Can we say five-alarm?
We know we got this.
So far we have been able to
handle the following:
***List all that went
well for you this morning.***

Evening Conversation:

Our wick is burning so
hot and bright.
What an amazing day.
We have to say we know the
following went well today.
***List all the positive
things you learned today. ***

We had trouble with the
following:
***List what provided a
challenge for you and how you
handled it.***

Additional Conversations:

When Faced With a Difficult Situation

We know this seems like a
serious challenge or block.
We can handle this. Take a
moment. Take a breath.
Let's center ourselves!
Take a look at all our options.
Look at our options. Which one
is best applied with the best
results? We can make the right
decision. We got this!

When you feel you can't do this

We knew this wasn't going to be
easy.
We chose to go down this road
for a reason.
We made the right choice.
You know that right? We got
this. We can push through this. We
got this!

Before Taking on too much

Okay! We want to help everyone.
We also want to go everywhere
   with all our friends.
If we do that when will we have
        time for us?
If we commit to this will we be
  over-extending ourselves?

When Faced With Doubt

We know that it's so much easier
        not to do this.
But we know that not doing this
   will not make us happy.
 We have become accustomed to
   looking in the mirror.
We love the person looking back
 at us. How can we go back?
 We can do this. We are better
   than we were yesterday.
     We refuse to go back.

Day 12

Some mornings can be a little bit more difficult than most. There are those mornings where it's just hard to get moving. These are the mornings when your self-talk and your inner dialogue are more crucial. These are the mornings that you have to speak joy and life into your mind. Into your heart. Into your day. Go and speak your joy into your day.

Daily Conversations:

Morning Conversation:

We are on fire!
We know that some days provide us with more challenges than most, but we are still pushing through this!
Why? Because we know what we are made of.
We know we have what it takes to

get through this day.
This and every day is our day.

Midday Conversation:

We hit a few bumps in the
road.
That is to be expected.
It's Okay. We still got this.
So far we have the following in
our favor:
***List all that went
well for you this morning.***

Evening Conversation:

Look at us today! We
rocked this day.
We know how great we were on
this day.
We can rest knowing that we got
so much done and learned so much.
***List all the positive
things you learned today. ***

There were a few
situations that proved a challenge
for us today.
***List what provided a
challenge for you and how you
handled it.***

Additional Conversations:

When Faced With a Difficult Situation

We know this seems like a
serious challenge or block.
We can handle this. Take a
moment. Take a breath.
Let's center ourselves!
Take a look at all our options.
Look at our options. Which one
is best applied with the best
results? We can make the right
decision. We got this!

When you feel you can't do this

We knew this wasn't going to be
easy.
We chose to go down this road
for a reason.
We made the right choice.
You know that right? We got
this. We can push through this. We
got this!

Before Taking on too much

Okay! We want to help everyone.

64

We also want to go everywhere
with all our friends.
If we do that when will we have
time for us?
If we commit to this will we be
over-extending ourselves?

When Faced With Doubt

We know that it's so much easier
not to do this.
But we know that not doing this
will not make us happy.
We have become accustomed to
looking in the mirror.
We love the person looking back
at us. How can we go back?
We can do this. We are better
than we were yesterday.
We refuse to go back.

Day 13

You have reached one of your luckiest days. Welcome to the lucky 13th day of getting to know you. You are one day closer to closing out your second week. Whoa! Your second week. Do you know what that means? You have committed to this for two whole weeks. How do you feel about yourself? Are you becoming more familiar with the person you are seeing in the mirror? Is your heart that much lighter? That much brighter? You should be so proud of yourself. You are thirteen days closer to feeling so much more comfortable in your skin. You are closer to you. This is a lucky day indeed.

Daily Conversations:

Morning Conversation:

Aren't we the lucky ones!
We opened our eyes this morning.
Look at that beautifully lucky
face.
Everything falls perfectly into
place on our face.
We woke up on this beautifully
wonderful day!
We got this! Let's go out there
and slay the day.

Midday Conversation:

We are feeling so lucky
today.
Everything is coming together.
So far today we got this done:
***List all that went
well for you this morning.***

Evening Conversation:

Every day feels like it
gets better and better.
Each day is better than the one
before.
We truly rocked today.
***List all the positive
things you learned today. ***

Despite our luck, we had

some issues with the following:
***List what provided a
challenge for you and how you
handled it.***

Additional Conversations:

When Faced With a Difficult
Situation

We know this seems like a
serious challenge or block.
We can handle this. Take a
moment. Take a breath.
Let's center ourselves!
Take a look at all our options.
Look at our options. Which one
is best applied with the best
results? We can make the right
decision. We got this!

When you feel you can't do this

We knew this wasn't going to be
easy.
We chose to go down this road
for a reason.
We made the right choice.
You know that right? We got

this. We can push through this. We
got this!

Before Taking on too much

Okay! We want to help everyone.
We also want to go everywhere
with all our friends.
If we do that when will we have
time for us?
If we commit to this will we be
over-extending ourselves?

When Faced With Doubt

We know that it's so much easier
not to do this.
But we know that not doing this
will not make us happy.
We have become accustomed to
looking in the mirror.
We love the person looking back
at us. How can we go back?
We can do this. We are better
than we were yesterday.
We refuse to go back.

Day 14

Congratulations to you! We have reached the end of our two weeks. I am going to ask you a few questions and I would suggest that you answer them in your journal today.

How do you feel about the person that you see in the mirror now?
What do like about him/her?
What don't you like about him/her?
What do you want to change?

Daily Conversations:

Morning Conversation:

Hello Gorgeous! We are SO ready for today.
Look at that beautiful body.

That body that houses us.
We are going to rock today.
We have no expectations for
today.
Just that we can take on what
comes our way.
All we have to do is bring our
"A" game.

Midday Conversation:

So far this has been a
good day.
Not completely perfect!
We already know there is no such
thing as the perfect day.
Yet we know we are still doing
well today because so far we have
this going for us.
***List all that went
well for you this morning.***

Evening Conversation:

Man! Not only did we make
it through this day but we have
reached our two-week mark.
We are beyond awesome.
***List all the positive
things you learned today. ***

Like any other day, some
issues had arisen.
Yet we have handled them the
best way that we could.
***List what provided a
challenge for you and how you
handled it.***

Additional Conversations:

When Faced With a Difficult
Situation

We know this seems like a
serious challenge or block.
We can handle this. Take a
moment. Take a breath.
Let's center ourselves!
Take a look at all our options.
Look at our options. Which one
is best applied with the best
results? We can make the right
decision. We got this!

When you feel you can't do this

We knew this wasn't going to be
easy.
We chose to go down this road

for a reason.
We made the right choice.
You know that right? We got
this. We can push through this. We
got this!

Before Taking on too much

Okay! We want to help everyone.
We also want to go everywhere
with all our friends.
If we do that when will we have
time for us?
If we commit to this will we be
over-extending ourselves?

When Faced With Doubt

We know that it's so much easier
not to do this.
But we know that not doing this
will not make us happy.
We have become accustomed to
looking in the mirror.
We love the person looking back
at us. How can we go back?
We can do this. We are better
than we were yesterday.
We refuse to go back.

Intermission #2

Like before, you can choose to use this day to take a break before moving forward. That is perfectly okay because you deserve it. Take a break and catch your breath. You have been spending the last two weeks opening a line of communication with yourself. Enjoy the real estate that you have reclaimed within your mind. On the same note, you have seen few things that you like as well. So let's take a personal assessment before moving forward:

List what you like/love about yourself

I like to always start with the positive because these traits are what will help you get through this next part. Remember that you are taking an honest look at yourself. You don't have to

share this with anyone you don't
choose to. With the positive, there
are those traits that are not so
positive. As you make this list
please take use a gentle but firm
hand with yourself.

List what you don't like about yourself

Now that you have your
list. Don't forget to include your
list from previous days. Now try to
answer the next few questions. Try
to be as honest as you can be with
yourself.

What can you change?
How can you change it?
How can you adjust to becoming
you that you know that you can be?

***Write out how you can adjust yourself to change the items that you don't like. ***

Now that you have made
your list, go and enjoy the you
that you have become so far. Go and
treat yourself to a dinner for one.
If that is too odd, then go and

spend some quality time with you.
Keep in mind that you are in charge
of the choices that you make. Know
that it's worth spending time with
you.

Day 15

Welcome to the beginning of the third week of your journey. I know that this adjustment has been a bit difficult. Yet if you take a moment to realize how wonderful it is to be that more familiar with that person in the mirror. It will take a bit of time to get past the uncomfortable part. Keep in mind that you are about to embark on your fifteenth day. You are halfway closer to being comfortable in your skin. Keep it up! You got this trooper. The next seven days are all you. The word "we" has now been replaced with "I". I know you can do this. You have made it this far.

Daily Conversations:

Morning Conversation:

Hello Beautiful! My hair
is too beautiful today.
Every strand is where it's
supposed to be.
I am so ready for today.
I know I got this because I am
wonderful.
Let's start this week right.

Midday Conversation:

Today is new and at the
same moment, it's not.
I know I am growing into the
person I know I am supposed to be.
I know this because of what I
have experienced so far.
I know this because of what I
have experienced.
***List all that went
well for you this morning.***

Evening Conversation:

This has been such an
empowering day.
I am empowered because I can see
who I am.
I brought life into who I am on
this day and every day.
Today I did the following

right:
***List all the positive
things you learned today. ***

I understand that there
is no such thing as a perfect day.
I accept all aspects of my day.
***List what provided a
challenge for you and how you
handled it.***

Additional Conversations:

When Faced With a Difficult Situation

I know this seems like a serious
challenge or block.
You can handle this. Take a
moment. Take a breath.
Center yourself!
Take a look at all your options.
Look at your options. Which one
is best applied with the best
results? You can make the right
decision. You got this!

When you feel you can't do this

You knew this wasn't going to be
easy.
You chose to go down this road
for a reason.
You made the right choice.
You know that right? You got
this. You can push through this.
You got this!

Before Taking on too much

Okay! I know you want to help
everyone.
You also want to go everywhere
with all your friends.
If you do that when will you
have time for yourself?
If your commitment to this will
you be over-extending yourself?

When Faced With Doubt

I know that it's so much easier
not to do this.
But I know that not doing this
will not make you happy.
I have become accustomed to
looking in the mirror.
I love the person looking back
at me. How can I go back?

I can do this. I am better than
I was yesterday.
I refuse to go back.

Day 16

There will be times that
challenge you. There will be times
that you can just brush it off.
Then will be times that you can
just brush it off. Then there will
be times when it will be more
difficult. You may be tempted
enough to fall back into the habits
that got you to where you were
fifteen days ago. Don't do it! As
you grow, you will be tested. You
will be tempted. It's all part of
the process of growth. Keep in mind
that YOU want this bad enough to
make it this far. You do have to
ask yourself. Do you want to go
back to where you were before day
one? When you feel yourself
slipping back adjust your self-talk
to keep you going. Know that you
got this.

Daily Conversations:

Morning Conversation:

Hello You! My eyebrows
are perfect.
Every strand.
I know I look too good for
today.
I am too hot to handle.
I have to finish getting ready
to face the world.
I got this!

Midday Conversation:

I am so killing it today.
All I need to know is that I am
in control of myself and how I
handle what comes at me.
***List all that went
well for you this morning.***

Evening Conversation:

I am so proud of myself.
I made it through this day.
I held my head high all day.
***List all the positive
things you learned today. ***

I also accept the things
that may have not gone the way I

wished they did.
***List what provided a
challenge for you and how you
handled it.***

Additional Conversations:

When Faced With a Difficult Situation

I know this seems like a serious
challenge or block.
You can handle this. Take a
moment. Take a breath.
Center yourself!
Take a look at all your options.
Look at your options. Which one
is best applied with the best
results? You can make the right
decision. You got this!

When you feel you can't do this

You knew this wasn't going to be
easy.
You chose to go down this road
for a reason.
You made the right choice.
You know that right? You got
this. You can push through this.

You got this!

Before Taking on too much

Okay! I know you want to help
everyone.
You also want to go everywhere
with all your friends.
If you do that when will you
have time for yourself?
If your commitment to this will
you be over-extending yourself?

When Faced With Doubt

I know that it's so much easier
not to do this.
But I know that not doing this
will not make you happy.
I have become accustomed to
looking in the mirror.
I love the person looking back
at me. How can I go back?
I can do this. I am better than
I was yesterday.
I refuse to go back.

Day 17

I hope you realize how wonderful you are in committing to yourself. You have found the time to invest in yourself. Do you know what this means? Do you realize how important you have become to you? How do you feel about yourself? You have rekindled a love affair with yourself. Keep it going.

Daily Conversations:

Morning Conversation:

I am so happy that I woke up today.
These eyes have opened to set sight on such beautiful things.
The first beautiful thing I see is me.
Today will be the day that I choose it to be.
I have to put my face on

and get this day going.

Midday Conversation:

I know not every day will
go my way.
I also know that not every
moment will go my way.
Yet I know there is always a ray
of light.
I know that just like the
sunshine on me,
I will shine a light on
everything within this day.
***List all that went
well for you this morning.***

Evening Conversation:

I am honestly happy with
how I handled it today.
Not every day is a rock and roll
day.
Yet every day has its Rock n
Roll moments.
***List all the positive
things you learned today. ***

I am willing to acknowledge the
shortcomings that I faced on this
day.

***List what provided a
challenge for you and how you
handled it. ***

Additional Conversations:

When Faced With a Difficult Situation

I know this seems like a serious
challenge or block.
You can handle this. Take a
moment. Take a breath.
Center yourself!
Take a look at all your options.
Look at your options. Which one
is best applied with the best
results? You can make the right
decision. You got this!

When you feel you can't do this

You knew this wasn't going to be
easy.
You chose to go down this road
for a reason.
You made the right choice.
You know that right? You got
this. You can push through this.
You got this!

Before Taking on too much

Okay! I know you want to help
everyone.
You also want to go everywhere
with all your friends.
If you do that when will you
have time for yourself?
If your commitment to this will
you be over-extending yourself?

When Faced With Doubt

I know that it's so much easier
not to do this.
But I know that not doing this
will not make you happy.
I have become accustomed to
looking in the mirror.
I love the person looking back
at me. How can I go back?
I can do this. I am better than
I was yesterday.
I refuse to go back.

Day 18

Chin up you! You are soaring with high moments. You are pushing through the low moments. You can handle it. No one has it easy all the time. Not every moment is guaranteed to be perfect. Yet every moment is guaranteed to be an experience. Every experience is an opportunity to grow and get better.

Daily Conversations:

Morning Conversation:

Who's that sexy thang
that I am looking at?
Who-Hoo!
I look too good.
I feel good.
Man! My nose is sitting
perfectly on my face.
Now I know I look good.
I am ready for today.

89

Midday Conversation:

So far so good.
Even as I am faced with the
bumps of the day, I know I am so
killing it today.
***List all that went
well for you this morning.***

Evening Conversation:

I have made it through
another beautiful day.
I love myself that much more
today.
This makes me feel so awesome.
***List all the positive
things you learned today. ***

Even the points of the
day that didn't go my way.
***List what provided a
challenge for you and how you
handled it.***

Additional Conversations:

**When Faced With a Difficult
Situation**

I know this seems like a serious

challenge or block.
You can handle this. Take a
moment. Take a breath.
Center yourself!
Take a look at all your options.
Look at your options. Which one
is best applied with the best
results? You can make the right
decision. You got this!

When you feel you can't do this

You knew this wasn't going to be
easy.
You chose to go down this road
for a reason.
You made the right choice.
You know that right? You got
this. You can push through this.
You got this!

Before Taking on too much

Okay! I know you want to help
everyone.
You also want to go everywhere
with all your friends.
If you do that when will you
have time for yourself?
If your commitment to this will
you be over-extending yourself?

When Faced With Doubt

I know that it's so much easier
not to do this.
But I know that not doing this
will not make you happy.
I have become accustomed to
looking in the mirror.
I love the person looking back
at me. How can I go back?
I can do this. I am better than
I was yesterday.
I refuse to go back.

Day 19

Welcome to another beautiful day! You should be truly proud of yourself. Look at how you have been pushing through. This is not a journey of solitude. If you are going through therapy I would recommend sharing any discoveries about yourself. It's natural to want to share our progress with others. I recommend starting in a safe place to assist in maintaining healthy boundaries.

Daily Conversations:

Morning Conversation:

I might be a little slow moving today but I know I can handle the day.
Oh, there we go!
My smile can get my day going at any time.
I still got this.

93

Midday Conversation:

I knew that I could make
it through this day.
I have accomplished so much so
far that proves to me that I can
make it through this day.
***List all that went
well for you this morning.***

Evening Conversation:

I have made it through
another day.
I am so loving this me.
This day has helped me see that
I am getting into the right
mindset.
I can make it through anything.
***List all the positive
things you learned today. ***

I love more themes that
can handle the down points of the
day:
***List what provided a
challenge for you and how you
handled it.***

Additional Conversations:

When Faced With a Difficult Situation

I know this seems like a true challenge. You can handle it. Take a breath. Center yourself!
Now take a good look at this situation. Look at your options. Which one is best applied with the best results? You got this!

When you feel you can't do this

You know that this isn't going to be easy. You chose to go down this road. You made the right choice.
You know that right? You got this. You can push through this. You got this!

Before Taking on too much

Okay! I know you want to help everyone and be everywhere with everyone.
When do you have time? Are you over-extending yourself?

When Faced With Doubt

I know that it's so much easier
not to do this.
But I know that not doing this
will not make you happy.
I have become accustomed to
looking in the mirror.
I love the person looking back
at me. How can I go back?
I can do this. I am better than
I was yesterday.
I refuse to go back.

Day 20

Did you realize that the kindness that you show to yourself spills over to those you interact with? The love you give yourself just spills into the world. You can't help but share your light with the world as you come closer to who you are.

Daily Conversations:

Morning Conversation:

Hello beautiful!
This is another wonderful day for me to take on.
I have a wonderful face to match what awaits me on this day.
I know I got this.

Midday Conversation:

I am feeling wonderful.
I have made it halfway through

this day.
I have so much to prove to me
how wonderful this day is.
***List all that went
well for you this morning.***

Evening Conversation:

This day proved to me
that I can make it through
anything.
I could see all the good that I
have experienced on this day.
***List all the positive
things you learned today. ***

I learned that I can
handle the obstacles that came my
way as well.
***List what provided a
challenge for you and how you
handled it.***

Additional Conversations:

When Faced With a Difficult Situation

I know this seems like a true
challenge. You can handle it. Take
a breath. Center yourself!

Now take a good look at this
situation. Look at your options.
Which one is best applied with the
best results? You got this!

When you feel you can't do this

You know that this isn't going
to be easy. You chose to go down
this road. You made the right
choice.
You know that right? You got
this. You can push through this.
You got this!

Before Taking on too much

Okay! I know you want to help
everyone and be everywhere with
everyone.
When do you have time? Are you
over-extending yourself?

When Faced With Doubt

I know that it's so much easier
not to do this.
But I know that not doing this
will not make you happy.
I have become accustomed to

looking in the mirror.
I love the person looking back
at me. How can I go back?
I can do this. I am better than
I was yesterday.
I refuse to go back.

Day 21

Congratulations on making it to the end of your final week. You have been rocking each day since you started. With every moment you have not just gotten closer to the you that you know. You have gotten better at being that person. Doesn't your back feel a bit straighter? Isn't your head held a bit higher? That is because of no one else but you. You believed in yourself enough to cause this beautiful evolution.

Daily Conversations:

Morning Conversation:

I am awesome.
Every week of these curves has made it through these last three weeks.
I love these curves.
I love me.
I love the theme that I am

becoming.

Midday Conversation:

I am so rocking it today,
so far.
This is why.
***List all that went
well for you this morning.***

Evening conversation:

I am so proud of myself
today.
I made it through the last day
of my three weeks.
***List all the positive
things you learned today. ***

I can handle my obstacles
better each day.
***List what provided a
challenge for you and how you
handled it.***

Additional Conversations:

**When Faced With a Difficult
Situation**

I know this seems like a true

challenge. You can handle it. Take
a breath. Center yourself!
Now take a good look at this
situation. Look at your options.
Which one is best applied with the
best results? You got this!

When you feel you can't do this

You know that this isn't going
to be easy. You chose to go down
this road. You made the right
choice.
You know that right? You got
this. You can push through this.
You got this!

Before Taking on too much

Okay! I know you want to help
everyone and be everywhere with
everyone.
When do you have time? Are you
over-extending yourself?

When Faced With Doubt

I know that it's so much easier
not to do this.
But I know that not doing this

will not make you happy.
I have become accustomed to
looking in the mirror.
I love the person looking back
at me. How can I go back?
I can do this. I am better than
I was yesterday.
I refuse to go back.

Intermission #3

Are you ready? I'm sorry I didn't hear you. Are you ready? You are about to embark on the last leg of this part of your journey. I say this part because you will keep evolving. I would suggest journaling the answers to the following questions:

- **How do you feel about that person in the mirror now, compared to when you started this journey?**
- **Are you more comfortable in your skin?**
- **Where would you like to grow?**

These questions are key to your future growth or shall I say you're familiar with who you are. I would like to share a wonderful piece of knowledge with you. So many people tend to look outside of themselves to find and/or define their desires and potential. During these past weeks, you have proven this theory to be wrong. How you may ask? The answer to that is quite simple. If you look back at the last three weeks. You dug deep within yourself and found more than what anything outside of yourself can provide. Give yourself a moment to take that in.

By now you should be in love with the person you see in the mirror. By now you may have realized some of the dreams that you may have abandoned or just forgot about. How you handled it was how you handled things in the past. You are now in the present. You can only deal with what you have before you. You have the tools to deal with those dreams differently. So this is your time to take inventory.

-        Where do you want to go?
-        How are you going to get there?

I highly encourage you to

take this day of intermission to
take all this into account before
you continue. Your time of union is
over. This is your time to mold you
know you can be.

Day 22

        You are so rocking this so far. You have been rocking it every day that you wake up and get out of bed. Every moment that you chose to wake up is one step closer for you to move forward and grow. How wonderful are you?

Daily Conversations:

Morning Conversation:

Hello Beautiful!
I am so happy with how beautiful my hair looks today.
I am so ready to be the me that I know I am.
Let's get this day going.

Midday Conversation:

        I am so happy that I have seen my strengths in action on this day.
So far I have discovered the

following about my strengths.
***List all that went
well for you this morning.***

Evening Conversation:

I beautifully enjoyed
myself today.
I enjoyed every interaction I
had today.
I especially enjoyed my
interaction with myself.
***List all the positive
things you learned today. ***

Even what has challenged
me today has helped me grow.
***List what provided a
challenge for you and how you
handled it.***

I have decided to work on
the following within my life:
***List all that you want
to change about yourself. ***

Additional Conversations:

When Faced With a Difficult Situation

I know this seems like a true
challenge. You can handle it. Take
a breath. Center yourself!
Now take a good look at this
situation. Look at your options.
Which one is best applied with the
best results? You got this!

When you feel you can't do this

You know that this isn't going
to be easy. You chose to go down
this road. You made the right
choice.
You know that right? You got
this. You can push through this.
You got this!

Before Taking on too much

Okay! I know you want to help
everyone and be everywhere with
everyone.
When do you have time? Are you
over-extending yourself?

When Faced With Doubt

I know that it's so much easier
not to do this.

But I know that not doing this
will not make you happy.
I have become accustomed to
looking in the mirror.
I love the person looking back
at me. How can I go back?
I can do this. I am better than
I was yesterday.
I refuse to go back.

Day 23

You should be so proud of yourself. Seriously, who is your number one fan? The correct answer to that question is you. Think about what you have accomplished in the last 22 days. You know that you are in a better headspace. This hasn't been an easy journey but it has been worth the tears and challenges. You are so far from being done but you are that much fortified within yourself.

Daily Conversations:

Morning Conversation:

I am too good for today.
I am so feeling myself right now.
Check out my beautiful eyebrows.
I will be the best I can be without interfering with anyone's path. Nor will I put others down.
I could be great and shine by

sharing my light with others.

Midday Conversation:

I have great potential.
I don't just know this, I have
witnessed this through my actions:
***List all that went
well for you this morning.***

Evening Conversation:

Today I feel that I know
who I am.
I also feel that I can build on
the theme that I see now.
I saw my brightness in the
following manner:
***List all the positive
things you learned today. ***

Every day I learn to
handle my challenges better.
***List what provided a
challenge for you and how you
handled it.***

I have come up with a
path to my goals
*** List your ways to
reach your goal.***

Additional Conversations:

When Faced With a Difficult Situation

I know this seems like a true challenge. You can handle it. Take a breath. Center yourself!
Now take a good look at this situation. Look at your options. Which one is best applied with the best results? You got this!

When you feel you can't do this

You know that this isn't going to be easy. You chose to go down this road. You made the right choice.
You know that right? You got this. You can push through this. You got this!

Before Taking on too much

Okay! I know you want to help everyone and be everywhere with everyone.
When do you have time? Are you over-extending yourself?

114

When Faced With Doubt

I know that it's so much easier
not to do this.
But I know that not doing this
will not make you happy.
I have become accustomed to
looking in the mirror.
I love the person looking back
at me. How can I go back?
I can do this. I am better than
I was yesterday.
I refuse to go back.

Day 24

There will be days when you hit a block. You will hit that wall. That is to be expected. Try to remember that there is nothing that is always easy. Things that provide you a certain level of difficulty give you a greater appreciation. Remember this when those times get almost too hard to bare. Or you think you can't keep going. The fire within you is too strong.

Daily Conversations:

Morning Conversation:

I am the spark that gets
this day going right.
My eyes are filled with
lightning.
I love my star-studded eyes.
I move at my own pace.
Get ready world, I'm bringing my
fire.

Midday Conversation:

I am just leaving a fiery
blaze in my wake.
I am inspired by everything
around me.
I also inspire those around me.
***List all that went
well for you this morning.***

Evening Conversation:

I am so proud of myself.
I handled this day like a true
champ.
I remember accomplishing the
following:
***List all the positive
things you learned today. ***

I am aware that every
champion has their trials.
***List what provided a
challenge for you and how you
handled it.***

I have gone the extra
mile.
***List the steps you're
taken to reach your goals.***

117

Additional Conversations:

When Faced With a Difficult Situation

I know this seems like a true challenge. You can handle it. Take a breath. Center yourself!
Now take a good look at this situation. Look at your options. Which one is best applied with the best results? You got this!

When you feel you can't do this

You know that this isn't going to be easy. You chose to go down this road. You made the right choice.
You know that right? You got this. You can push through this. You got this!

Before Taking on too much

Okay! I know you want to help everyone and be everywhere with everyone.
When do you have time? Are you over-extending yourself?

When Faced With Doubt

I know that it's so much easier
not to do this.
But I know that not doing this
will not make you happy.
I have become accustomed to
looking in the mirror.
I love the person looking back
at me. How can I go back?
I can do this. I am better than
I was yesterday.
I refuse to go back.

Day 25

You are wonderful! Do you truly realize how wonderful you are? You are not wonderful in just being you. Your actions are what make you wonderful. You are wonderful with the energy that you release into the world. It is that wonderfulness that you have been spilling into the world. Keep up the good work.

Daily Conversations:

Morning Conversation:

Hello, Wonderful! I am so happy that I woke up today.
It just helps to love my nose for detail.
Not only did I wake up but I woke up ready to bring my "A" game.

Midday Conversation:

I am so happy with how I

handled myself today.
I can see the following good
things so far:
***List all that went
well for you this morning.***

Evening Conversation:

I am happy with how I
handled myself on this day.
I was able to see all the
wonderful aspects of my day.
***List all the positive
things you learned today. ***

I am also proud of how I
handled the challenges of the day.
***List what provided a
challenge for you and how you
handled it.***

Additional Conversations:

When Faced With a Difficult Situation

I know this seems like a true
challenge. You can handle it. Take
a breath. Center yourself!
Now take a good look at this
situation. Look at your options.

Which one is best applied with the best results? You got this!

When you feel you can't do this

You know that this isn't going to be easy. You chose to go down this road. You made the right choice.
You know that right? You got this. You can push through this. You got this!

Before Taking on too much

Okay! I know you want to help everyone and be everywhere with everyone.
When do you have time? Are you over-extending yourself?

When Faced With Doubt

I know that it's so much easier not to do this.
But I know that not doing this will not make you happy.
I have become accustomed to looking in the mirror.
I love the person looking back

at me. How can I go back?
I can do this. I am better than
I was yesterday.
I refuse to go back.

Day 26

Normally we would start the celebration of the coming of another week. Since we are just five days away from the end of your thirty days, we are going to push through to the end. If you need an intermission to feel free to take one. If there is any takeaway from this, you should be able to know when you need to take time for yourself. If there is anything the last twenty-five days have taught you is that time for you is essential.

Morning Conversation:

Hello, Wonderful! Look at that wonderful face.
Everything on this face is exactly where it should be.
I know I am wonderfully motivated.
I know I am wonderfully kind.
I know I am wonderful in every moment.
I know I am wonderful with every

interaction that I will have today.

Midday Conversation:

I am having such a
wonderful day.
I have set my own pace and I
have been rewarded for it.
***List all that went
well for you this morning.***

Evening Conversation:

I have to say that today
was a wonderful day.
Today I showed myself just how
wonderful I can be.
I stepped up to the plate.
***List all the positive
things you learned today. ***

I was even able to deal
with my challenges wonderfully.
***List what provided a
challenge for you and how you
handled it.***

I have taken the following steps
toward my goals.
***List what provided a
challenge for you and how you

handled it.***

Additional Conversations:

When Faced With a Difficult Situation

I know this seems like a true challenge. You can handle it. Take a breath. Center yourself!
Now take a good look at this situation. Look at your options. Which one is best applied with the best results? You got this!

When you feel you can't do this

You know that this isn't going to be easy. You chose to go down this road. You made the right choice.
You know that right? You got this. You can push through this. You got this!

Before Taking on too much

Okay! I know you want to help everyone and be everywhere with everyone.
When do you have time? Are you

over-extending yourself?

When Faced With Doubt

I know that it's so much easier
not to do this.
But I know that not doing this
will not make you happy.
I have become accustomed to
looking in the mirror.
I love the person looking back
at me. How can I go back?
I can do this. I am better than
I was yesterday.
I refuse to go back.

Day 27

As you go through every day and every moment, you will be faced with the unfortunate fact the outside world is obsessed with the bottom line. Remember that no amount can sum up your actual worth. You are priceless. Yes! You are priceless. Look into that mirror and look at the most priceless thing in the world.

Daily Conversations:

Morning Conversation:

Every day I have felt more and more like the person I am more familiar with.
I know these curves.
I love these curves.
Today I am moving that much closer to the person that I know I can be.

Midday Conversation:

I am so proud of the

progress that I have made today.
I am so hitting the mark.
***List all that went
well for you this morning.***

Evening Conversation:

Every day I make
progress.
No matter how small the
progress.
It's still progress.
***List all the positive
things you learned today. ***

Even the things that
cause me frustration help me in my
progress.
***List what provided a
challenge for you and how you
handled it.***

Additional Conversations:

When Faced With a Difficult Situation

I know this seems like a true
challenge. You can handle it. Take
a breath. Center yourself!
Now take a good look at this

situation. Look at your options.
Which one is best applied with the
best results? You got this!

When you feel you can't do this

You know that this isn't going
to be easy. You chose to go down
this road. You made the right
choice.
You know that right? You got
this. You can push through this.
You got this!

Before Taking on too much

Okay! I know you want to help
everyone and be everywhere with
everyone.
When do you have time? Are you
over-extending yourself?

When Faced With Doubt

I know that it's so much easier
not to do this.
But I know that not doing this
will not make you happy.
I have become accustomed to
looking in the mirror.

I love the person looking back
at me. How can I go back?
I can do this. I am better than
I was yesterday.
I refuse to go back.

Day 28

You are so close to the person that can take on the world again. You must be so proud of yourself. In the last 27 days, you have grown so much. Many take years to get where you have gotten to. You have put in the work. You are almost there. Keep up the great work.

Daily Conversations:

Morning Conversation:

Hello! I am so ready for today.
I understand that every day will have its challenges.
I am so ready for this day and any challenges that come with it.

Midday Conversation:

I accept the obstacles that have been placed before me so far.
I have made a full effort to

understand them.
No matter what happens I can
always find my sunshine.
***List all that went
well for you this morning.***

Evening Conversation:

I am so proud of how I
handled the challenges that I was
faced with today.
***List all the positive
things you learned today. ***

Even the ones that cause
me to put extra thought.
***List what provided a
challenge for you and how you
handled it.***

Additional Conversations:

When Faced With a Difficult Situation

I know this seems like a true
challenge. You can handle it. Take
a breath. Center yourself!
Now take a good look at this
situation. Look at your options.
Which one is best applied with the

best results? You got this!

When you feel you can't do this

You know that this isn't going
to be easy. You chose to go down
this road. You made the right
choice.
You know that right? You got
this. You can push through this.
You got this!

Before Taking on too much

Okay! I know you want to help
everyone and be everywhere with
everyone.
When do you have time? Are you
over-extending yourself?

When Faced With Doubt

I know that it's so much easier
not to do this.
But I know that not doing this
will not make you happy.
I have become accustomed to
looking in the mirror.
I love the person looking back
at me. How can I go back?

I can do this. I am better than
I was yesterday.
I refuse to go back.

Day 29

How do you feel about yourself right now? You are only one day away from reaching your goal at this point of the journey. Hold your head up high. Your commitment and dedication have gotten you this far. You should be so proud of yourself. You didn't only commit but you committed to the most important person in the world. YOU!

Daily Conversations:

Morning Conversation:

Hello Super Star! Yeah, I said it, I'm a Super Star. I'm going toward this day like a Super Star.
I got this.

Midday Conversation:

This star is shining brighter than I was earlier today. I know this because I

accomplished the following so far
today:
***List all that went
well for you this morning.***

Evening Conversation:

I want to sing on high
how much of a Superstar I am.
This day has been one of the
best.
All because I was able to do the
following:
***List all the positive
things you learned today. ***

I was able to rock the
aspects of the day that were a bit
more challenging.
***List what provided a
challenge for you and how you
handled it.***

Additional Conversations:

When Faced With a Difficult Situation

I know this seems like a true
challenge. You can handle it. Take
a breath. Center yourself!

Now take a good look at this
situation. Look at your options.
Which one is best applied with the
best results? You got this!

When you feel you can't do this

You know that this isn't going
to be easy. You chose to go down
this road. You made the right
choice.
You know that right? You got
this. You can push through this.
You got this!

Before Taking on too much

Okay! I know you want to help
everyone and be everywhere with
everyone.
When do you have time? Are you
over-extending yourself?

When Faced With Doubt

I know that it's so much easier
not to do this.
But I know that not doing this
will not make you happy.
I have become accustomed to

138

looking in the mirror.
I love the person looking back
at me. How can I go back?
I can do this. I am better than
I was yesterday.
I refuse to go back.

Day 30

OMG! I am so happy for you. You have reached the last day of this part of your journey. You have made the journey and you have reached the end of this leg. You are too fabulous for words. You deserve to celebrate this achievement. Hopefully, this has motivated you to mold the rest of your journey.

Daily Conversations:

Morning Conversation:

I am so proud of myself for making it to this point. I have made it to 30 days. I know this is not the end of my journey. I know that this is just the beginning. I am giving this my all.

Midday Conversation:

Every day that passes I

have learned such wonderful things
about myself.
I know who I truly am.
***List all that went
well for you this morning.***

Evening Conversation:

I have come to the end of
my 30 days.
This is not an end but it's
truly a new beginning for me.
Today has helped me place the
final brick with my foundation.
***List all the positive
things you learned today.***

I will always know with
every good day I will still be
faced with challenges.
***List what provided a
challenge for you and how you
handled it.***

Additional Conversations:

When Faced With a Difficult Situation

I know this seems like a true
challenge. You can handle it. Take

a breath. Center yourself!
Now take a good look at this
situation. Look at your options.
Which one is best applied with the
best results? You got this!

When you feel you can't do this

You know that this isn't going
to be easy. You chose to go down
this road. You made the right
choice.
You know that right? You got
this. You can push through this.
You got this!

Before Taking on too much

Okay! I know you want to help
everyone and be everywhere with
everyone.
When do you have time? Are you
over-extending yourself?

When Faced With Doubt

I know that it's so much easier
not to do this.
But I know that not doing this
will not make you happy.

I have become accustomed to
looking in the mirror.
I love the person looking back
at me. How can I go back?
I can do this. I am better than
I was yesterday.
I refuse to go back.

Hello [Insert Name Here]

Congratulations! You have made it to the end of your 30 days. How do you feel? When you look in the mirror do you recognize the person looking back?

Despite that this is the end of this thirty-day venture. By no means is this the end of your journey. If you think about it, you just finished packing the bags and placed them in the car for your trip. You got everything that you may deem necessary for your next step. As you take a seat behind the wheel you will begin to see infinite roads of possibilities that you can take.

From this point, you can continue to build on the person that you know you can be. Have you set a plan and a counter plan with the direction that you have chosen to take. Either way, you have your foundation. You have a building block that you didn't have 30 days

ago. Don't lose sight of yourself.
Keep growing. Go and search out
what keeps that spark going within
you.

Made in the USA
Middletown, DE
06 October 2022

11978285R00086